Robert Louis Stevenson's

TREASURE ISLAND
Student Guide

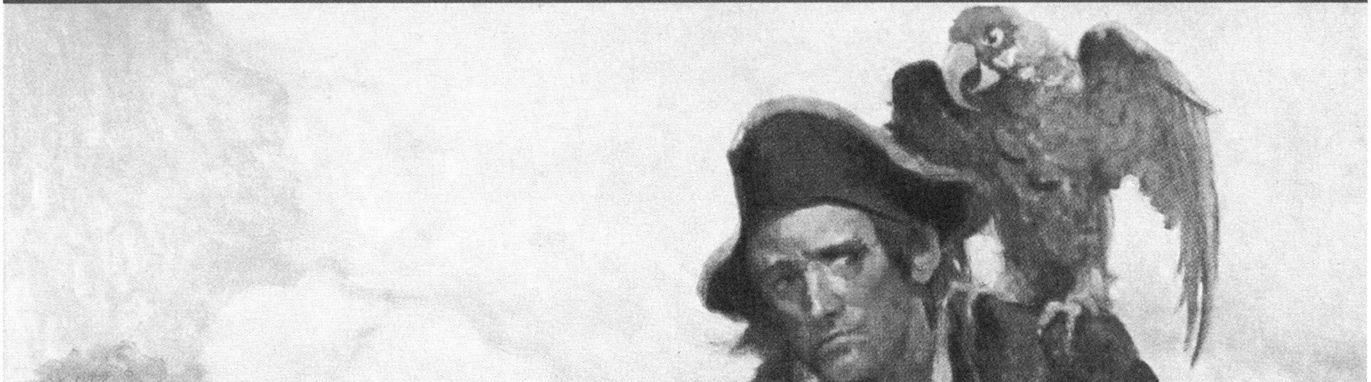

MEMORIA PRESS

Memoria Press

www.MemoriaPress.com

Robert Louis Stevenson's
TREASURE ISLAND

STUDENT GUIDE

Contributing Editors: Cheryl Lowe, Jennifer Farrior, and Sean Brooks

ISBN 978-1-61538-070-1

First Edition © 2010 Memoria Press Copyright, LLC | 1123

Contents

PREPARING TO READ:

REVIEW

- Orally review any previous vocabulary.
- Review the plot of the book as read so far.
- Periodically review the concepts of character, setting, and plot.

STUDY GUIDE PREVIEW

- Reading Notes:
  - Read aloud together.
  - This section gives the student key characters, places, and terms that are relevant to a particular time period, etc.
- Vocabulary:
  - Read aloud together so that students will recognize words when they come across them in their reading.
  - Look at each word within the context that it is used, and help your student come up with the best synonym that defines the word. (Make sure it is a synonym the student knows the meaning of.)
  - Record the word's meaning in the students' study guides. (Use students' knowledge of Latin and other vocabulary to decipher meanings.)
- Comprehension Questions:
  - Read through these questions with students to encourage purposeful reading.

READING:

- Student reads the chapter (or selection of the chapter for that lesson) independently or to the teacher (for younger students).
- For younger students, you can alternate between teacher-read and student-read passages. Model good reading skills. Encourage students to read expressively and smoothly. The teacher may occasionally take oral reading grades.
- While reading, mark each vocabulary word as you come across it.
- Have students take note in their study guide margin of pages where a Comprehension Question is answered.

AFTER READING:

COMPREHENSION QUESTIONS

- Older students can answer these questions independently, but younger students (2nd-4th) need to answer the questions orally, form a good sentence, and then write it down, using correct punctuation, capitalization, and spelling. (You may want to write the sentence down for the younger student after forming it orally, and then let the student copy it perfectly.)
- It is not necessary to write the answer to every question; some may be better answered orally. Just make sure you answer the questions that will appear on tests so that students will have the information they need to study.
- Answering questions and composing answers is a valuable learning activity. Questions require students to think; writing a concise answer is a good composition exercise.

QUOTATIONS AND DISCUSSION QUESTIONS

- Use the Quotations and Discussion Questions section of each lesson as a guide to your oral discussion of the key concepts in the chapter that may not be covered in the comprehension questions.
- These talking points can take your oral discussion to a higher level than covered in the students' written work. Use this time as an opportunity to introduce higher-level thinking. You can introduce concepts the students may not be mature enough to fully understand yet but that would be beneficial for them to begin thinking about.
- A key to the Discussion Questions is in the back of the *Teacher Guide*.

ENRICHMENT

- The Enrichment activities include composition, copywork, dictation, research, mapping, drawing, poetry work, literary terms, and more.
- This section has a variety of activities in it, but the most valuable activity is composition. Your student should complete at least one composition assignment each week. Proof student's work and have student copy composition until grammatically perfect. Insist on clear, concise writing. For younger students, start with 2-3 sentences, and do the assignment together. The student can form good sentences orally as you write them down, and then the student copies them.
- These activities can be completed as time and interest allow. Do not feel you need to complete all of these activities. Choose the ones that you feel are the best use of your students' time.

UNIT REVIEW AND TESTS

- There is a unit review and a quiz or test following every few lessons (varies by individual guide).
- On the weeks that have these reviews and tests, you may want to do the review early in the week, and then drill it orally a couple of times before giving the test at the end of the week.
- A final comprehensive test is also included.

Robert Louis Stevenson (1850-1894) was born in Edinburgh, Scotland. Although Stevenson suffered from tuberculosis, which caused his early death at age forty-four, he did not let his physical weaknesses hinder him from living an adventurous life.

As he was often bed-ridden with his illness, Stevenson began at an early age to entertain himself by making up stories.

This passion for creating a world apart from his own did not stop as he entered his adult life, despite his family's attempt to discourage him. In 1867 he entered the University of Edinburgh to study engineering, for his family's profession was lighthouse design. However, he had no desire for his studies, and spent more energy in creating friendships with his fellow students.

In 1871 Stevenson announced to his father that he was not fit to be an engineer and would pursue life as a writer.

He gained inspiration for his stories as he traveled around the world, despite uncomfortable and even dangerous means, and risking his health besides. His adventures included pursuing his future wife halfway around the world, being suspected as a spy by the French police, and immersing himself in the culture of the South Pacific islands, amongst what most people of the time would have called savage cannibals.

When *Treasure Island* was published in the 1880s, it was extremely popular among children and adults alike. Even in Stevenson's time, pirates were not at all common, so he decided to set his story during the 1700s, and used strange words to give the story an older feel.

After battling sickness and depression later in life, Stevenson bounced back to write what he felt was his best work, *Weir of Hermiston*; however, he died before he could complete it.

While Stevenson was wildly popular in his day, the rise of modern literature after the first World War lowered his reputation to a second-class writer, and he suffered criticism by other notable literary figures, such as Virginia Woolf. Regardless, Stevenson has been admired by Ernest Hemingway, Rudyard Kipling, and G. K. Chesterton, among many others.

To this day, Stevenson remains very popular, and is ranked the 25th most translated author in the world, ahead of fellow nineteenth-century writers Charles Dickens, Oscar Wilde, and Edgar Allan Poe.

Some of Stevenson's other works include *Kidnapped*, *A Child's Garden of Verses*, and *The Strange Case of Dr. Jekyll and Mr. Hyde*.

Robert Louis Stevenson is an example of how following your true passion, despite sickness, opposition, and criticism, can truly be rewarding. And we are rewarded with the opportunity to partake in swashbuckling adventure in the fantastic world he created within the pages of *Treasure Island*.

Reading Notes

Jim Hawkins	the narrator of the story; young boy
Dr. Livesey	the doctor who tends to Jim's father; confronts the captain
Admiral Benbow	the name of the inn that Jim's father runs
the captain/Billy Bones	the old seaman with a scar on his cheek who lodges at the inn
Black Dog	a seaman missing two fingers; looking for Bill at the inn

Vocabulary
Write the meaning of each bold word or phrase.

1. the **sabre** cut across one cheek, a dirty, **livid** white _______________________________

2. he drank slowly, like a **connoisseur** _______________________________

3. seemed like a **mate** or **skipper** _______________________________

4. a thousand **diabolical** expressions _______________________________

5. wringing his hands after such a **rebuff** _______________________________

6. the **ruffian** had told him _______________________________

7. if it's only for a piece of **incivility** like tonight's _______________________________

8. a pale, **tallowy** creature _______________________________

9. half **fawning**, half **sneering** _______________________________

10. exposed his great **sinewy** arm _______________________________

Comprehension Questions
Answer the following in complete sentences.

1. What does the captain ask Jim to do for him? How much does he pay Jim for this? _______________

____

____

2. What haunts Jim's dreams? Describe these dreams. _______________________________

____

____

____

3. Contrast Dr. Livesey and the captain. Why is Dr. Livesey able to humiliate the captain who had terrorized everyone else? Where is Dr. Livesey mentioned before this encounter? _______________

    ____

    ____

    ____

    ____

    ____

4. Why does Black Dog come to the inn, and what is the captain's reaction to him? _______________

    ____

    ____

    ____

5. What happens between Black Dog and the captain when Jim leaves the room? _______________

    ____

    ____

    ____

Quotations

Identify the speaker of the following.

"I'm a plain man; rum and bacon and eggs is what I want." _______________________________________

"Silence, there, between decks!" ____

"Ah, Bill, Bill, we have seen a sight of times, us two …" _______________________________________

"If it comes to swinging, swing all, say I." ____

"I clear my conscience—the name of rum for you is death." _______________________________________

Discussion Questions

1. Describe the old seaman. Does he fit the description of a pirate? Why or why not?
2. Why do you think this particular dream keeps haunting Jim? Have you ever been haunted by something in a dream?
3. Would you call Black Dog and the captain friends? Why or why not?
4. What was Dr. Livesey's advice to the captain? Do you agree with this advice?

Reading Notes

the blind beggar   the man who delivers the black spot to the captain; walks with a stick

Vocabulary

Write the meaning of each bold word or phrase.

1. That's a **summons**, mate. ____

2. He **clambered** up and down stairs___________________________________

3. his temper was more **flighty** _______________________________________

4. gripped it in a moment like a **vice** _________________________________

5. It **cowed** me more than the pain. ___________________________________

6. The captain had been struck dead by thundering **apoplexy**. ___________

Comprehension Questions

Answer the following in complete sentences.

1. How does the captain get Jim to bring him some rum? What does he ask Jim to do for him if he can't "get away nohow"? ____

    ____

    ____

    ____

2. What keeps Jim busy and distracts him from worrying about the captain? ___________

    ____

    ____

    ____

3. Describe the captain's behavior as he grows sicker. ______________________________

    ____

    ____

    ____

    ____

4. Who comes to visit the captain? Describe him. _______________________________________

____

____

____

5. How does the captain react to this visitor? What happens between them?_______________

____

____

____

____

6. What is Jim's reaction to the captain's collapse? ____________________________________

____

____

____

Quotations

Identify the speaker of the following.

"Doctors is all swabs." ____

"Now, if I can't get away nohow, and they tip me the black spot ..." ____________________

"Take me in straight or I'll break your arm." ____

"If I can't see, I can hear a finger stirring." ____

Discussion Questions

1. What is the "black spot"?

2. What does the captain mean when he says rum has been "meat and drink, and man and wife" to him?

Reading Notes

Captain Flint   the name that carried a great weight of terror with the people

Vocabulary
Write the meaning of each bold word or phrase.

1. that **detestable** blind beggar____

2. They say cowardice is **infectious**; but then argument is, on the other hand, a great **emboldener**.

   ____

3. Overcoming a strong **repugnance** _______________________________________

4. Under that, the **miscellany** began _______________________________________

5. I'll show these **rogues** that I'm an honest woman. _______________________

6. **obstinately** unwilling ____

Comprehension Questions
Answer the following in complete sentences.

1. What do Jim and his mother immediately do after Jim tells his mother all that he knows about the captain? ____

   ____

   ____

2. Describe the reaction of the people in the neighboring hamlet to their situation. _______________

   ____

   ____

   ____

   ____

3. What is Jim's mother's response to them?_______________________________________

   ____

   ____

   ____

4. What does Jim find when he searches the captain's body for the key to the chest? _______________

   ____

   ____

   ____

   ____

5. What does the fact that the captain collected seashells from West India tell us about him?

____

____

____

____

Quotations
Identify the speaker of the following.

"Back we will go, the way we came, and small thanks to you big, hulking, chicken-hearted men."

____

"He had till ten, Mother." ____

"I'll have my dues, and not a farthing over." _______________________________

"And I'll take this to square the count." _______________________________

Discussion Questions

1. Why does Jim blame his mother for both "her honesty and her greed"? Do you agree with him?

Enrichment

1. Research and write a report on the various types of coins found in the captain's sea-chest: *doubloons*, *louis d'ors*, *guineas*, and *pieces of eight*.

Reading Notes

Pew	the blind beggar
Dirk	one of Pew's men, whom he calls a fool and a coward
Supervisor Dance	police officer who arrives to investigate

Vocabulary
Write the meaning of each bold word or phrase.

1. the **formidable** beggar ____

2. **Rout** the house out! ____

3. the rest stood **irresolute** on the road_______________________________________

4. you stand there **skulking** ____

5. the blind **miscreant** ____

6. she still continued to **deplore** the balance _______________________________

Comprehension Questions
Answer the following in complete sentences.

1. What does Jim see when he looks back at the inn? _______________________________

____

____

2. Pew and his men don't care about Captain Bones' money. What motivates them to find his chest?

____

____

____

3. Who else, according to Pew's last words, is involved in the plot? ___________________

____

4. What happens to Pew at the end of the chapter? _______________________________

____

____

5. What does Jim find when he goes back to the inn? What does he think about this? ______________

____

____

____

____

6. What does Jim tell Supervisor Dance? ____

____

____

Quotations

Identify the speaker of the following.

"Budge, you skulk!" ____

"Oh, shiver my soul, if I had eyes!" ____

"If you had the pluck of a weevil in a biscuit you would catch them still." ______________

"I'm glad I trod on Master Pew's corns." ____________________________________

"I believe I have the thing in my breast pocket." ______________________________

Discussion Questions

1. What do you think would have happened if the officers had not arrived when they did?

2. What is "Flint's fist"?

Enrichment

1. Draw a picture of the inn after Pew and his men ransack it.

Squire Trelawney landowner who finances the treasure hunt

Vocabulary
Write the meaning of each bold word or phrase.

1. a **bluff**, rough-and-ready face _______________________________________

2. says he, very stately and **condescending** _______________________________

3. close-cropped black **poll** ____

4. This lad Hawkins is a **trump**, I perceive. _________________________________

5. The Spaniards were so **prodigiously** afraid of him__________________________

6. But you are so **confoundedly** hot-headed ________________________________

Comprehension Questions
Answer the following in complete sentences.

1. Dr. Livesey and the squire discuss Flint and his treasure. What do they know about Flint?

    ____

    ____

    ____

    ____

2. Describe what is inside Flint's oilskin packet.______________________________

    ____

    ____

    ____

3. Describe the squire's proposed treasure hunt. How is Jim to be included? ___________

    ____

    ____

    ____

    ____

    ____

                                                                 Chapter 6

4. What cause for concern does Dr. Livesey have about the treasure hunt? Why? ________________

____

____

____

____

5. What is the squire's response to Dr. Livesey's fear?

____

____

Quotations

Identify the speaker of the following.

"Hawkins has earned better than cold pie." ____

"Heard of him! Heard of him, you say!" ____

"Thrifty man! He wasn't the one to be cheated." ____

"I'll be as silent as the grave." ____

Discussion Questions

1. What do you think about the squire's attitude regarding the treasure hunt?

2. Do you believe what the squire says in response to Dr. Livesey's fear? Why or why not?

Enrichment

1. Bury or hide something in your backyard or house. Then draw a map leading to its location,
   including landmarks, such as trees or furniture. Have a parent or friend try to find your "treasure"
   using your map.

Drawing Page

Reading Notes

Tom Redruth	the elderly gamekeeper at the Hall, temporarily in charge of Jim
Hispaniola	the name of the ship Trelawney bought for the expedition
Blandly	an old friend of Trelawney's who sold him a ship; joins the crew

Vocabulary
Write the meaning of each bold word or phrase.

1. I **brooded** by the hour ____

2. the most **transparent calumnies** ___________________________________

3. wanted a good **berth** as cook _______________________________________

4. the most **indomitable** spirit ____

5. a **capital** imitation of a sailor's walk ________________________________

Comprehension Questions
Answer the following in complete sentences.

1. Where does Jim stay while waiting for the treasure hunt preparations to be completed? How does
    he pass the time? ____

    ____

    ____

    ____

2. What about Trelawney's letter worries Jim? ___________________________

    ____

    ____

    ____

3. How did Trelawney find his crew in Bristol? What makes you think the squire was gullible?

    ____

    ____

    ____

    ____

    ____

    ____

4. What makes Jim think about the home that he is leaving? How does he react to this? ___________

____

____

____

____

5. What is one of Jim's last thoughts before leaving home? ___________________________

____

____

____

6. What delights Jim upon his arrival to Bristol? _________________________________

____

____

____

Quotations

Identify the speaker of the following.

"The squire has been talking, after all." ____

"A pretty rum go if squire ain't to talk for Dr. Livesey, I should think." ___________________

"Imagine the abominable age we live in!" ____

"Sail! We sail tomorrow!" ____

Discussion Questions

1. What qualities would you look for in crew members if you were in the squire's position?

2. What does Trelawney mean when he describes Long John Silver as "a man of substance"?

3. Do you agree with how Jim treats the apprentice boy? What would you have done differently?

Enrichment

1. Draw a picture of the *Hispaniola*, the schooner (definition in the index) bought by the squire.

Reading Notes

Long John Silver	the tall, strong, one-legged sailor hired as a cook for the crew
Tom Morgan	an old sailor who was drinking with Black Dog in the tavern
Spy-glass	the tavern where Jim meets Long John Silver

Vocabulary
Write the meaning of each bold word or phrase.

1. he managed with wonderful **dexterity**. ___________________________________

2. then, **relinquishing** my hand ___________________________________

3. came forward pretty sheepishly, rolling his **quid** ___________________________________

4. we laughed together, **peal** after peal ___________________________________

5. I was again obliged to join him in his **mirth**. ___________________________________

6. telling me some little **anecdote** of ships ___________________________________

Comprehension Questions
Answer the following in complete sentences.

1. Describe Jim's meeting with Long John Silver. Give references to Silver and his character. ________
   ____
   ____
   ____
   ____
   ____

2. Who did Jim originally fear Long John Silver might be? ___________________________________
   ____
   ____
   ____
   ____

3. What pirate does Jim see in the Spy-glass? What is Silver's reaction? ___________________________________
   ____
   ____
   ____
   ____

4. What is Jim's opinion of Long John Silver? _______________________________

    ____

    ____

    ____

5. What is the reaction of Dr. Livesey and Squire Trelawney to Silver's story? _______________

    ____

    ____

    ____

Quotations
Identify the speaker of the following.

But he was too deep, and too ready, and too clever for me. _______________________________

"… you're as smart as paint." _______________________________

"Why, shiver my timbers." _______________________________

"The man's a perfect trump." _______________________________

Discussion Questions

1. Are you surprised that Jim so easily trusts Long John Silver? Why or why not?

2. Why do you think Jim says Silver is "one of the best possible shipmates"?

Reading Notes

Captain Smollett   sharp-looking captain of the *Hispaniola*; disliked by the squire

Mr. Arrow   the ship's mate; brown old sailor; friends with the squire

Vocabulary
Write the meaning of each bold word or phrase.

1. all **shipshape** and **seaworthy**?____

2. I was **engaged**, sir, on what we call **sealed orders** ________________________

   ____

   ____

3. Now, treasure is **ticklish** work. ______________________________________

4. but the **slight**, if there be one, was unintentional. __________________________

5. make a **garrison** of the stern part of the ship______________________________

   ____

6. In other words, you fear a **mutiny**. ____________________________________

Comprehension Questions
Answer the following in complete sentences.

1. What are Captain Smollett's complaints? __________________________________

   ____

   ____

   ____

2. Compare the reactions of Squire Trelawney and Dr. Livesey to the captain's complaints.

   ____

   ____

   ____

   ____

   ____

   ____

3. What does Captain Smollett request? Is this done?__________________________

   ____

   ____

   ____

Chapter 9

4. How does Jim feel about the captain? Why? _______________________________________

____

____

____

Quotations

Identify the speaker of the following.

"Well, sir, better speak plain … I don't like this cruise; I don't like the men; and I don't like my officer. That's short and sweet." _______________________________________

"… I'll tell you my way of it—life or death, and a close run." _______________________________________

"Contrary to all my notions, I believe you have managed to get two honest men on board with you—that man and John Silver." _______________________________________

"… as for that intolerable humbug, I declare I think his conduct unmanly, unsailorly, and downright un-English."

____

Discussion Questions

1. Do you agree with Squire Trelawney or Dr. Livesey in regard to Captain Smollett? Why?

Enrichment

1. Read Aesop's fable "A Mountain in Labor." Copy this fable onto another piece of paper, and write a paragraph explaining what Dr. Livesey means when he compares Captain Smollett's errand and misgivings to it.

Reading Notes

Job Anderson	the boatswain who takes over as mate after Arrow disappears
Israel Hands	the coxswain; experienced seaman; confidant of Silver
Barbecue	the crew's nickname for Long John Silver

Vocabulary
Write the meaning of each bold word or phrase.

1. And then the whole crew **bore** chorus____

2. he began to appear on deck with **hazy** eye ____

3. he carried his crutch by a **lanyard** round his neck ________________________________

4. I seen him **grapple** four ____

5. the dishes hanging up **burnished** ____

6. the last day of our outward voyage by the largest **computation** ___________________

Comprehension Questions
Answer the following in complete sentences.

1. What carries Jim back to the Admiral Benbow "in a second"? Why?_____________________

____

____

2. Describe Mr. Arrow's character. What happens to him? _____________________

____

____

____

3. How does Long John Silver move about on the ship? What is the general opinion of him by the crew? What does the coxswain tell Jim about Silver? _____________________

____

____

____

____

____

4. Does Captain Smollett have a change of heart regarding his original complaints? Explain.

____

____

____

5. How does the apple barrel prove to be significant? _______________________________

____

____

Quotations

Identify the speaker of the following.

"He's no common man, Barbecue." _______________________________________

"Pieces of eight! pieces of eight! pieces of eight!" _______________________________

"She'll lie a point nearer the wind than a man has a right to expect of his own married wife, sir."

____

"A trifle more of that man, and I shall explode." _______________________________

Discussion Questions

1. What does Silver mean when he says, "You can't touch pitch and not be mucked"?

Enrichment

1. Find on a world map the places that Silver's parrot has traveled: Madagascar, Malabar, Surinam, Providence, Portobello, and Goa.

2. Find the definitions of the following nautical terms: *coxswain* (in index), *grog*, *duff*, *the trades* (in index), *bowsprit* (in index), *helm* (in index), *luff* (in index).

Reading Notes

Dick the crew's youngest hand; Jim overhears him speaking with Silver

Vocabulary
Write the meaning of each bold word or phrase.

1. asked Silver **derisively** ____

2. Dick's **square.** ____

3. you was a kind of a **chapling**, John ____
____

4. Put 'em ashore like **maroons**? ____
____

5. Don't you get sucking of that **bilge**, John. ____
____

6. You fill a **pannikin** and bring it up. ____

Comprehension Questions
Answer the following in complete sentences.

1. Whom does Jim overhear talking while he's in the apple barrel? What are they discussing?
____
____
____
____

2. What is said that hurts Jim's feelings? What is his reaction to this? ____
____
____
____

3. What becomes clear about Silver's relationship to Pew and Flint? ____
____
____
____

4. What is Silver's plan? ____
____
____
____

Chapter 11

5. What does Dick question about the plan? What is Silver's response? Why? _______________

____

____

____

____

6. What is Silver's one request about the plan? _____________________________________

____

7. How does Jim know that there are still innocent men on board? _______________________

____

____

____

Quotations

Identify the speaker of the following.

"But now, you look here: you're young, you are, but you're as smart as paint. I see that when I set my eyes on you, and I'll talk to you like a man." ____

"I didn't half a quarter like the job till I had this talk with you, John; but there's my hand on it now."

____

"You'll have your mouthful of rum tomorrow, and go hang." ____________________________

"Dooty is dooty, mates. I give my vote—death." ____________________________________

Discussion Questions

1. What is a "gentleman of fortune"?

2. What does the phrase "Dead men don't bite" mean?

Enrichment

1. Draw a picture of the scene with Jim in the apple barrel. Include details.

2. Silver mentions "Execution Dock." Research what he is referencing.

Drawing Page

Reading Notes

Skeleton Island   the name of the land in sight; a main place for pirates at one time

Spy-glass   the main hill on the island, where the pirates kept a look-out

Capt. Kidd's Anchorage   the name of the anchorage on the island

Vocabulary
Write the meaning of each bold word or phrase.

1. There all hands were already **congregated**. _______________________________________

2. if such was your intention as to enter and **careen** _________________________________

3. the **coolness** with which John **avowed** his knowledge _____________________________

____

4. I had … taken such a **horror** of his cruelty, **duplicity**, and power ___________________

____

5. then make some **pretence** to send for me ____

6. The doctor changed **countenance** a little ____

____

Comprehension Questions
Answer the following in complete sentences.

1. How does Jim know that Silver will be disappointed by the map the captain pulls out?

____

____

2. What surprises Jim about Silver? ____

____

____

____

3. After Jim tells the squire, the doctor, and the captain about what he overheard, what do they immediately do? ____

____

____

____

4. What is each of their responses to this news? _________________________________

____

____

____

____

5. What are the captain's three points? _______________________________________

____

____

____

6. How do the men feel about Jim's role in this situation? How does Jim feel about this? Why?

____

____

____

____

Quotations

Identify the speaker of the following.

"He'd look remarkably well from a yard-arm, sir." _______________________________

"You, sir, are the captain. It is for you to speak." _______________________________

"And to think that they're all Englishmen! Sir, I could find it in my heart to blow the ship up."

____

"Hawkins, I put prodigious faith in you." _______________________________________

Discussion Questions

1. What does the captain mean when he says Silver would "look remarkably well from a yard-arm"?

2. How would you feel if you were in Jim's position at the end of the chapter?

Vocabulary

Write the meaning of each bold word or phrase.

1. The Spy-glass … was likewise the strangest in **configuration** ______________________

   ____

2. the whole ship creaking, groaning, and jumping like a **manufactory** __________________

   ____

3. I never learned to stand without a **qualm** or so ________________________________

4. A peculiar **stagnant** smell hung over the anchorage ______________________________

5. the birds once more flying and **squalling** around the anchorage ____________________

   ____

Comprehension Questions

Answer the following in complete sentences.

1. Describe the island. ____

   ____

   ____

   ____

   ____

2. The crew is ready to mutiny. What does the captain have in mind when he says Silver is their "one man to rely on"? What advantage does Silver have in keeping the peace? __________________

   ____

   ____

   ____

   ____

   ____

3. What is the crew's reaction after the captain suggests they go ashore? What is behind Captain Smollett's decision not to protest? ____

   ____

   ____

   ____

   ____

   ____

Chapter 13

4. What is Jim's spontaneous decision? Does he regret it? Explain why or why not. _______________

____

____

____

____

Quotations
Identify the speaker of the following.

"I don't know about treasure, but I'll stake my wig there's fever here." _______________________

"Is that you, Jim? Keep your head down." ____

"Jim, Jim!" ____

Discussion Questions

1. The doctor says he smells fever on the island, and the whole crew seems to have caught the "infection" of mutiny. Why does the author so closely use the analogies of fever and infection when referring to Treasure Island?

2. Do you like or dislike the fact that occasionally Jim informs the reader about the ultimate outcomes of his decisions? Why or why not?

Enrichment

1. Draw a picture of Jim in the boat heading to the island.

2. Find the definitions of the following nautical terms: *scupper*, *boom* (in index), *block*, *warp*, *pike*, *gig* (in index).

Reading Notes

Tom   the honest seaman; killed by Silver

Alan   another honest seaman; screams out when killed by the mutineers

Vocabulary
Write the meaning of each bold word or phrase.

1. an open piece of **undulating**, sandy country ____

2. raising my head to an **aperture** among the leaves ______________________________________

3. disturbed the **languor** of the afternoon ____

4. Tom lay motionless upon the **sward**. ____

5. several **modulated** blasts ____

6. Instantly I began to **extricate** myself and crawl back __________________________________

____

Comprehension Questions
Answer the following in complete sentences.

1. What is Jim's initial emotion after escaping into the island? Why? ____________________

____

____

____

2. Whom does Jim overhear conversing? What are they saying? ________________________

____

____

____

3. What interrupts this conversation? ____

____

____

4. What follows as a result from this conversation? ________________________________

____

____

____

____

5. What is Jim's reaction to this turn of events? Explain in detail. ______________________

____

____

____

____

Quotations

Identify the speaker of the following.

"If I hadn't took to you like pitch, do you think I'd have been here a-warning of you?"

____

"It's a black conscience that can make you feared of me." _______________________________

"Then rest his soul for a true seaman!" ____

"If I die like a dog, I'll die in my duty." ____

Discussion Questions

1. To which animals does the author/Jim compare Silver? What other words are used in the place of
    Silver's name, labeling him? What effect does this have on the reader?

Enrichment

1. Research rattlesnakes. Write a short paper on their physical characteristics, habitat, eating habits,
    and why they are so dangerous.

Reading Notes

| **Ben Gunn** | marooned on the island for three years; former member of Flint's crew |

Vocabulary
Write the meaning of each bold word or phrase.

1. the terror of this new **apparition** brought me to a stand ______________________________

    ____

2. behind me the murderers, before me this lurking **nondescript**.______________________________

    ____

3. a system of the most various and **incongruous** fastenings______________________________

    ____

4. brass buttons, bits of stick, and loops of **tarry gaskin** ______________________________

    ____

5. leather belt, which was the one thing solid in his whole **accoutrement**.______________________________

    ____

6. The cannon-shot was followed … by a **volley** of small arms ______________________________

    ____

Comprehension Questions
Answer the following in complete sentences.

1. What is it that makes Silver appear "less terrible" to Jim? Why? ______________________________

    ____

    ____

    ____

2. Who is Ben Gunn? Describe him. ______________________________

    ____

    ____

    ____

    ____

3. Why does Ben Gunn want to come with Jim on board the ship? ______________________________

    ____

    ____

    ____

Chapter 15

4. What connects Ben Gunn with Silver and the treasure?

____

____

____

____

____

____

5. What does Ben Gunn tell Jim to say about him to the others? _______________________

____

____

____

Quotations

Identify the speaker of the following.

"If ever I can get aboard again, you shall have cheese by the stone." _______________________

"… you'll bless your stars, you will, you was the first that found me!" _______________________

"If you was sent by Long John, I'm as good as pork, and I know it." _______________________

"Now, I'll tell you what. So much I'll tell you, and no more. I were in Flint's ship when he buried the treasure."

Discussion Questions

1. Ben Gunn believes that Providence put him there on the island. What does he mean by this? Do you agree with him?

2. What do you think Ben Gunn means when he says he puts more confidence in a gentleman born than a gentleman of fortune?

Enrichment

1. Ben Gunn refers to the game of "chuck-farthen." Find out how to play this game, then play it with your classmates.

2. When Ben Gunn says to Jim, "You're all in a clove hitch, ain't you?" he's metaphorically referring to a type of knot. Research this knot. Then find a piece of rope, and see if you can tie it yourself.

Reading Notes

John Hunter	one of Squire Trelawney's men
Richard Joyce	one of Squire Trelawney's men
Abraham Gray	one of the ship's crew; joins up with the captain and his men

Vocabulary

Write the meaning of each bold word or phrase.

1. If ever a man smelt fever and **dysentery**, it was in that abominable anchorage.

    ____

    ____

2. it was in that **abominable** anchorage _______________________________________

3. in the direction of the **stockade** upon the chart. ______________________________

    ____

    ____

4. the thing was completed by a **paling** six feet high ______________________________

5. they might have held the place against a **regiment**. _____________________________

6. tossed our stores over the **palisade**. ____

Comprehension Questions

Answer the following in complete sentences.

1. What makes the doctor's pulse go "dot and carry one" (skip a beat)? Why? ___________________

    ____

    ____

    ____

2. Why is the doctor not worried about going back to the ship for a second load of provisions? Why do they dump the remainder of the weapons and ammunition overboard? ___________________

    ____

    ____

    ____

3. Describe how Smollett handles Gray. _______________________________________

    ____

    ____

    ____

Chapter 16

4. How does Captain Smollett discover Gray's loyalty? _______________________________

____

____

____

5. Why is Smollett so anxious to bring Gray ashore? _______________________________

____

____

____

Quotations

Identify the speaker of the following.

"There's a man … new to this work. He came nigh-hand fainting, doctor, when he heard the cry. Another touch of the rudder and that man would join us." _______________________________

"I know you are a good man at bottom, and I dare say not one of the lot of you's as bad as he makes out."

____

"I'm risking my life and the lives of these good gentlemen every second." _______________________________

"I'm with you, sir." ____

Discussion Questions

1. Why does the author switch the narrative to the doctor's perspective in this chapter? Is this confusing or interesting? Explain.

2. What does the incident between Smollett and Gray further reveal about Smollett's character?

Enrichment

1. Research the system of bells used during the sailors' watches. In the first line of this chapter, the doctor says, "It was about half past one—three bells in the sea phrase." How much time has gone by on the watch?

2. Draw a picture of the stockade, using the details given in the chapter.

Vocabulary

Write the meaning of each bold word or phrase.

1. the little **gallipot** of a boat ____

2. The **gunwale** was lipping astern. ______________________________________

3. He looked to the **priming** of his gun. ______________________________________

4. The ebb-tide … was now making **reparation** and delaying our **assailants.** ____________

____

____

5. The other three took complete **headers**, and came up again______________________

____

6. he had carried his over his shoulder by a **bandoleer**______________________________

____

7. he had not uttered one word of surprise, complaint, fear, or even **acquiescence** __________

____

8. We had no **ricochet** to fear. ____

9. Silver was in the **stern-sheets** in command. ______________________________

Comprehension Questions

Answer the following in complete sentences.

1. How does the captain's well-planned course of action suddenly go awry? ________________

____

____

____

2. Why is the doctor concerned about Hunter and Joyce standing firm at the stockade? __________

____

____

____

3. What happens to Redruth? How does the squire react?______________________________

____

____

____

Chapters 17-18

4. What does the captain insist on doing? And how does this "foolishness" prove to be a wise course of action?____

____

____

____

____

____

5. What do the men find when they go out to retrieve the provisions that fell into the water when their jolly-boat sank? ____

____

____

Quotations
Identify the speaker of the following.

"Carpet bowls! My lady's maid couldn't miss." _______________________________________

"Be I going, doctor?" ____

"It mayn't be good divinity, but it's a fact." ____

"Strike my colours! No, sir, not I." ____

Discussion Questions

1. The squire was useless on the ship, but then proves to be a deadly shot. What causes the sudden change in the squire?

2. Redruth is described as laying "like a Trojan" behind his mattress. What is meant by this reference?

Enrichment

1. Research what a *long nine* is. Draw a detailed picture.

2. Make your own flag to hang in your room.

Reading Notes

Jolly Roger   the black flag of pirates; usually depicted with a skull and crossbones

Union Jack   the national flag of the United Kingdom

Vocabulary
Write the meaning of each bold word or phrase.

1. Reasons of his own; that's the **mainstay**. ______________________________________

2. the wood still **flourished** high and dense ______________________________________

3. towards the sea with a large **admixture** of live-oaks. ______________________________

4. I was put **sentry** at the door. ______________________________________

5. And you never saw me take **snuff**. ______________________________________

6. each had a good **stiff** glass of brandy______________________________________

Comprehension Questions
Answer the following in complete sentences.

1. Why doesn't Ben Gunn go with Jim into the stockade? What are the "reasons of his own"?

____

____

____

____

2. What does Captain Smollett do to keep everyone from being depressed? ________________

____

____

____

____

3. What does the doctor tell Jim he will give to Ben Gunn? Why?________________________

____

____

____

4. What is the group's "best hope" for survival?________________________________

____

____

____

5. What are the group's "two able allies"? Explain. __________________________

____

____

____

Quotations
Identify the speaker of the following.

"You're a good boy, or I'm mistook; but you're on'y a boy, all told." ________________________

"That man Smollett is a better man than I am. And when I say that it means a deal, Jim."

____

"A man who has been three years biting his nails on a desert island, Jim, can't expect to appear as sane as you or me." ________________________

*"First ship that ever I lost."*____

Discussion Questions

1. What is the Jolly Roger? What is the Union Jack? What is their significance?

2. What does it mean that the doctor "staked his wig"?

Enrichment

1. Draw a picture of the Jolly Roger and the Union Jack.

2. Write a short essay on how the general opinion of Captain Smollett has changed since the beginning of the voyage. Include specific examples.

Vocabulary

Write the meaning of each bold word or phrase.

1. Silver himself, standing **placidly** by.___________________________

2. crawled during the night out of the **morass**. ___________________________

3. seeing how **cavalier** had been the captain's answer.___________________________

4. He had been growing **nettled** before___________________________

5. I'll give you my **affy-davy**, upon my word of honor___________________________
____

6. Growling the foulest **imprecations**___________________________

7. the **resin** melting in the logs of the block house.___________________________
____

8. "Thank you, sir," returned Joyce with the same quiet **civility**.___________________________
____

9. with a loud **huzza**, a little cloud of pirates leaped from the woods___________________________

10. as the blow still hung **impending** ___________________________

11. When I had first **sallied** from the door ___________________________

12. at any moment the fire might **recommence**. ___________________________

Comprehension Questions

Answer the following in complete sentences.

1. What caused Silver to come seeking a truce? What does Jim have an "inkling" about?
____
____
____
____

2. What are the terms of Silver's truce? ___________________________
____
____
____

3. What is the captain's response to Silver's terms? ___________________________
____
____
____

4. Describe the reversal of positions Jim mentions. _______________________________________

____

____

5. Who wins the battle, and what is the price they had to pay for their victory? By how many men are they now outnumbered? ____

____

Quotations

Identify the speaker of the following.

"Cap'n, is it? My heart, and here's promotion!" _______________________________________

"And what's more I would see you and him and this whole island blown clean out of the water into blazes first."

____

"Laugh, by thunder, laugh! Before an hour's out, ye'll laugh upon the other side. Them that die'll be the lucky ones." _______________________

"I thought you had worn the king's coat!" _______________________________________

"At 'em, all hands—all hands!" _______________________________________

"Round the house, lads! Round the house!" _______________________________________

Discussion Questions

1. Who do you think is more confident of his group at the end of Chapter 20—Captain Smollett or Silver? Explain.

2. What do you think will be the final outcome of the battle? Why?

Enrichment

1. Write a paragraph explaining what Captain Smollett means when he says, "I'll see you all to Davy Jones."

Vocabulary

Write the meaning of each bold word or phrase.

1. I took the first step towards my **escapade** _______________________________

    ____

2. I was to go … **ascertain** whether it was there or not _______________________

3. a certain tossing of **foliage** and grinding of boughs _______________________

4. Ben Gunn's boat … was like the first and the worst **coracle** ever made by man. _______________

    ____

5. you would have thought I had had enough of **truantry** for once. _______________

    ____

6. I had taken another **notion** ____

7. the mutineers, after their **repulse** of the morning _________________________

8. the defeated pirates lay **carousing** in the swamp. _________________________

    ____

Comprehension Questions

Answer the following in complete sentences.

1. Where does Jim believe the doctor is heading? _____________________________

    ____

    ____

2. What is it that overcomes Jim almost as strong as fear? What does this cause him to feel and do?

    ____

    ____

    ____

    ____

    ____

    ____

3. As Jim gets closer to the mutineers, what sound does he hear? What is the source of this sound?

____

____

____

____

4. What is Jim's plan? ______________________________________

____

____

5. What are the "two points" visible to Jim on the whole anchorage? ______________

____

____

Quotations

Identify the speaker of the following.

"Well, shipmate, mad he may not be; but if he's not, you mark my words, I am!" ______________

Discussion Questions

1. Jim called leaving the stockade his "second folly," far worse than his first; and yet at the same time he mentioned it would help in saving them. Explain this paradox. Have you ever experienced making a big mistake that turned out to be "providential"?

2. Do you think Jim has a good plan? Do you think it will succeed? Why or why not? If in his position, what would you do?

Enrichment

1. Draw a picture of Ben Gunn's boat, as described in the book.

2. Find the definitions of the following nautical terms in the index: *bulwarks, thwart.*

Vocabulary

Write the meaning of each bold word or phrase.

1. turning round and round was the **manoeuvre** she was best at. _______________

   ____

2. a ditty rather too **dolefully** appropriate _______________________________

3. all these buccaneers were as **callous** as the sea they sailed on. _______________

4. just as I gave the last **impulsion**, my hands came across a light cord _______________

5. little ripples, combing over with a sharp, bristling sound and slightly **phosphorescent**._________

   ____

6. until sleep at last **supervened**____

7. loud **reverberations** … succeeded one another from second to second _______________

   ____

8. spending my strength in vain to scale the **beetling crags**. _______________

   ____

9. there was no **contrariety** between [the wind] and the current _______________

   ____

10. I saw I must **infallibly** miss that point _______________________________

11. I felt sure I should make the next **promontory** without fail. _______________

   ____

Comprehension Questions

Answer the following in complete sentences.

1. What does Jim remember prior to cutting the rope that attaches the ship to the anchor? How does
   this change his course of action? _______________________________________

   ____

   ____

2. How and why does Jim decide to take a look through one of the cabin windows? What does he see?

   ____

   ____

   ____

3. How does Jim react to his impending doom at the end of Chapter 23? _______________

____

____

____

____

____

4. Explain Jim's strategy to maneuver the coracle. ___________________________

____

____

____

____

5. What does Jim think when he sees the *Hispaniola* at sea? What does this lead him to plan?

____

____

____

Quotations

Identify the speaker of the following.

"But one man of her crew alive,

What put to sea with seventy-five." _____________________________________

"Clumsy fellows, they must still be drunk as owls." ___________________________

Discussion Questions

1. Did you know what Jim was planning when he went in search of Ben Gunn's coracle? Was his mission a success? Why or why not?

Enrichment

1. Find the definitions of the following nautical terms: *hawser* (in index), *yaw*, *skiff*, *billows*, *tiller* (in index), *tack* (in index), *forefoot* (in index), *jib-boom* (in index), *stay*, *swell*.

Drawing Page

Reading Notes

O'Brien   the seaman with the red cap; killed by Israel Hands

Vocabulary
Write the meaning of each bold word or phrase.

1. the ship kept bucking and **sidling** like a vicious horse

2. the whole body **canting** towards the stern

3. the lamp still cast a smoky glow, **obscure** and brown as **umber**.

4. **Foraging** about, I found a bottle with some brandy left

5. Why, I ain't sich an **infernal** lubber, after all.

6. I was greatly **elated** with my new command

7. my conscience, which had **smitten** me hard for my desertion

8. a **haggard** old man's smile; but there was, besides that, a grain of **derision**

Comprehension Questions
Answer the following in complete sentences.

1. Describe the state of the *Hispaniola* as Jim finds it.

2. What are the emotions going through Jim at the state of Israel Hands?

3. What bargain does Jim strike with Israel Hands? _______________________________

____

____

4. How does Jim feel about his new position? _________________________________

____

____

____

____

5. Explain the foreboding in the last sentence of this chapter. _______________________

____

____

____

____

Quotations

Identify the speaker of the following.

"Brandy." ____

"I don't have no manner of luck, you see, and that's what's the matter with me."

____

"I've come aboard to take possession of this ship, Mr. Hands; and you'll please regard me as your captain until further notice." ____

"God save the king! And there's an end to Captain Silver!"

____

Discussion Questions

1. Why do you think Jim waits to give the brandy to Israel until after he's had a good, deep drink of water himself?

2. Why does Jim say, "Better none than these" when taking down the Jolly Roger?

3. What is your impression of Israel Hands? Do you think Jim made a good bargain with him?

Vocabulary
Write the meaning of each bold word or phrase.

1. The whole story was a **pretext**.

2. I think I was a good, prompt **subaltern**

3. the space was longer and narrower and more like … the **estuary** of a river

4. we saw the wreck of a ship in the last stages of **dilapidation**.

5. had not a sudden **disquietude** seized upon me

6. his face itself as red as a red **ensign** with his haste and fury.

7. a moment or two passed in **feints** on his part

8. We were both of us **capsized** in a second

9. I scarce can say it was by my own **volition**

Comprehension Questions
Answer the following in complete sentences.

1. Describe how Jim finds out that Israel Hands is planning on killing him.

2. When Israel Hands complains about dying, what does Jim advise him to do? What is Hands' response to this, and how does Jim react?

3. Why does Jim feel confident about his stance against Hands, even after his guns initially do not work?

4. What weakness in Jim almost becomes his downfall? Explain.________________________________

____

____

____

5. What is the outcome of the battle? ____

____

____

Quotations

Identify the speaker of the following.

"You can kill the body, Mr. Hands, but not the spirit; you must know that already." ________________

"I'm for my long home, and no mistake." ____

"Jim, I reckon we're fouled, you and me, and we'll have to sign articles." ________________________

Discussion Questions

1. How does Jim know that the coxswain is lying when he says he prefers wine to brandy?

2. Why do you think the author ended the chapter the way he did?

Enrichment

1. What is Israel Hands' philosophy of life? Write a few sentences explaining it.

Vocabulary
Write the meaning of each bold word or phrase.

1. I **desisted** with a violent shudder._______________________________________

2. nor did it greatly **gall** me when I used my arm. _______________________________

3. he lay like some horrible, **ungainly** sort of puppet ___________________________

4. the strain was so heavy that I half feared to **meddle**. _________________________

5. I walked more **circumspectly**, keeping an eye on every side. ___________________
    ____

6. I slacked my pace and went a **trifle warily**. _________________________________
    ____

7. they kept an **infamous** bad watch ____

Comprehension Questions
Answer the following in complete sentences.

1. What is Jim afraid of, more than the pain in his shoulder?______________________
    ____
    ____

2. Describe Jim's emotions as he sets out to find his friends. ______________________
    ____
    ____
    ____
    ____

3. What does he see on his way? What does he assume it is? ______________________
    ____
    ____
    ____

4. What causes wonder and terror in Jim as he nears the camp? What puts him back at ease?

____

____

____

____

5. Describe what happens once Jim is inside the camp. _________________________________

____

____

____

____

____

Quotations
Identify the speaker of the following.

"Pieces of eight! Pieces of eight! Pieces of eight! Pieces of eight!" _______________________________

"Who goes?" ____

Discussion Questions

1. Which apprehensions should Jim have heeded when heading back to camp?

2. Where do you think Jim's friends are?

Enrichment

1. Create your own scenario where Jim escapes capture.

2. Write a one-page description of your scenario and share with the class.

Vocabulary
Write the meaning of each bold word or phrase.

1. The parrot sat, **preening** her plumage _______________________________

   ____

2. stick the **glim** in the wood heap _______________________________________

3. I stood there, looking Silver in the face, **pluckily** enough _______________

   ____

4. the cabin party were **incensed** at me for my desertion _________________

5. cried Silver **truculently** ____

6. his eye kept wandering **furtively** _______________________________________

7. I know a lad that's **staunch**. ____

Comprehension Questions
Answer the following in complete sentences.

1. What does Silver tell Jim about his friends? How does Jim feel about this information?

   ____

   ____

   ____

   ____

   ____

2. How does Jim respond when Silver asks him to choose to join his men or be on his own, and what
   does he offer? ____

   ____

   ____

3. How do the men respond to Silver when he comes to Jim's defense after Morgan wants to kill him?

   ____

   ____

   ____

   ____

4. Describe Silver's plan involving Jim. What does Jim begin to understand? _______________

   ____

   ____

   ____

Chapter 28

5. What does Silver reveal to Jim at the end of the chapter? _______________________________

____

____

Quotations

Identify the speaker of the following.

"The laugh's on my side; I've had the top of this business from the first." _______________________________

"Cross me, and you'll go where many a good man's gone before you …" _______________________________

"But, you mark, I stand by you through thick and thin." _______________________________

"What I can do, that I'll do." _______________________________

Discussion Questions

1. Describe Jim's relationship with Silver.

2. Do you think Jim made a good decision regarding his deal with Silver? Why or why not?

Enrichment

1. Research what Silver means by telling his men, "P'r'aps you can understand King George's English."

2. Find the meanings of the following terms used in the narrative's context: *rum puncheon, marlin-spike, caulker.*

George Merry   buccaneer with yellow eyes; accuses Silver of ruining the trip

Vocabulary
Write the meaning of each bold word or phrase.

1. this **emissary** retired again _______________________________

2. I won't hurt a **depytation**. _______________________________

3. you don't be under no kind of **apprehension** _______________________________

4. he had been talking with a **vehemence** that shook the house. _______________________________

5. you, George Merry, that had the **ague shakes** upon you not six hours agone _______________________________

6. the dark perils that **environed** _______________________________

Comprehension Questions
Answer the following in complete sentences.

1. What do the buccaneers return with for Silver? _______________________________

2. What are George's four grievances against Silver? _______________________________

3. What is Silver's response to these grievances? _______________________________

4. What does Silver reveal? How do the buccaneers respond? _______________________________

____

____

____

5. What does Jim think about as he falls asleep? ____

____

____

____

____

____

Quotations

Identify the speaker of the following.

"The black spot! I thought so." ____

"You're a funny man, by your account; but you're over now ..." ___________________________

"We'll all swing and sun-dry for your bungling." _______________________________________

"Barbecue forever! Barbecue for cap'n!" ____

Discussion Questions

1. What was Silver trying to do by pointing out the fact that the men had used a page from the Bible to deliver the black spot?

2. Has your opinion of Silver changed at all?

Enrichment

1. Silver again refers to "Execution Dock by London town." If you did not research this reference from Chapter 11, do so now. Share your findings with the class.

Drawing Page

Vocabulary
Write the meaning of each bold word or phrase.

1. I remembered with confusion my **insubordinate** and stealthy conduct. _______________

2. not having sense enough to know … the dry land from a vile, **pestiferous slough**. _______

3. you don't appear to me to have the **rudiments** of a notion_______________

4. his last night's victory had given him a huge **preponderance** on their minds. _____________

5. till then I'll **gammon** that doctor, if I have to ile his boots with brandy._______________

6. silenced by his **volubility** rather than convinced. _______________

Comprehension Questions
Answer the following in complete sentences.

1. When the doctor comes to the mutineers' camp, how does he treat them? How do the mutineers respond to their guest?_______________

2. Of what do the mutineers accuse Silver? Are they right or wrong?_______________

3. How does Silver gain back his crew's loyalty?_______________

4. Why is Jim not afraid of death? What is it that Jim *is* afraid of? _______________________

____

____

____

5. What deal does the doctor strike with Silver? ____

____

____

Quotations

Identify the speaker of the following.

"Block house, ahoy! Here's the doctor." ____

"I make it a point of honour not to lose a man for King George (God bless him!) and the gallows."

____

"Doctor, I'm no coward; no, not I—not so much!" _______________________________________

"There is a kind of fate in this." ____

Discussion Questions

1. Why does the doctor tell Jim, "There is a kind of fate in this"? Do you agree?
2. Do you admire Jim for keeping his word to Silver? What would you have done?

Enrichment

1. Of what do the words *forfeit*, *perjury*, and *concession* remind you? Is there significance behind the author using these terms?

Reading Notes

Flint's Pointer/Allardyce   the skeleton of one of Flint's crew; points the way to the treasure

Vocabulary
Write the meaning of each bold word or phrase.

1. Should the scheme he had now sketched prove **feasible**_______________________________

____

2. their inexplicable **cession** of the chart____

3. The other men were variously **burthened**, some carrying picks and shovels _______________

____

4. his mutineers … must have been driven to **subsist** on clear water and the proceeds of their hunting.

____

5. it was not likely they would be very **flush** of powder. ___________________________________

____

6. the terms of the note on the back … admitted of some **ambiguity**.__________________________

____

7. the rough, cliffy **eminence** called the Mizzen-mast Hill._________________________________

Comprehension Questions
Answer the following in complete sentences.

1. Describe Jim's impression of the mutineers over breakfast, including Silver. _________________

____

____

____

2. How does Silver act over breakfast? ____

____

____

____

3. What are Jim's misgivings regarding Silver? regarding his friends? ________________________

____

____

____

____

____

4. What problem do the mutineers encounter as they use Flint's chart to hunt the treasure?

____

____

____

____

5. What do they discover? What is their reaction? ___________________________________

____

____

____

____

Quotations

Identify the speaker of the following.

"… we'll save our necks in spite o' fate and fortune." _______________________________

"Look out for squalls when you find it." _______________________________________

"Dear heart, but he died bad, did Flint!" _____________________________________

"Care killed a cat. Fetch ahead for the doubloons." __________________________________

Discussion Questions

1. What does living "hand to mouth" mean?

2. What do you think the doctor's warning to Silver, "Look out for squalls when you find it," means?

Enrichment

1. Make your own replica of Flint's chart, including the note on the back. Be as detailed as possible.

2. Research the type of food sailors had to eat. What is *junk*?

Vocabulary
Write the meaning of each bold word or phrase.

1. it's someone **skylarking**—someone that's flesh and blood _______________________________

    ____

2. growing terror at the **irreverence** of his words. ____

3. It was **conspicuous** far to sea both on the east and west ___________________________________

4. Before us was a great **excavation** ____

5. All was clear to **probation**. ____

6. The **cache** had been found and **rifled**. ____

    ____

    ____

Comprehension Questions
Answer the following in complete sentences.

1. "I never have seen men more dreadfully affected than the pirates. The colour went from their six
    faces like enchantment; some leaped to their feet, some clawed hold of others; Morgan grovelled
    on the ground." What is the cause of this commotion? Of what are the men convinced? Why?

    ____

    ____

    ____

    ____

    ____

2. What does Silver say that upsets Merry? Then what does he say that calms the men down?

    ____

    ____

    ____

    ____

    ____

    ____

3. Describe the change in the pirates when they near the treasure. ______________________________

    ____

    ____

    ____

    ____

4. What does Jim think about Silver's changed attitude? What does he imagine Silver might do?

____

____

____

____

5. What waits for the pirates where the treasure should be? ____________________

____

____

Quotations

Identify the speaker of the following.

"Fetch aft the rum, Darby!" ____

"I'll not be beat by man nor devil." _______________________________________

"Don't you cross a sperrit." ____

"Why, nobody minds Ben Gunn; dead or alive, nobody minds him." __________________

Discussion Questions

1. Whose voice do you think was the voice among the trees? Why?

2. Why does Merry say that nobody minds Ben Gunn, dead or alive?

3. Did it surprise you that the nearness of treasure changed the mutineers' attitude?

Enrichment

1. Give your best impression of the ghostly voice.

Write the meaning of each bold word or phrase.

1. I was so **revolted** at these constant changes_______________________________

2. I could not **forbear** whispering _______________________________

3. "Dig away, boys," said Silver, with the coolest **insolence**._______________________________

4. [they] were already **ambushed** before the arrival of the treasure-hunters._______________________________
   ____

5. you're a **prodigious** villain and impostor _______________________________

6. It is a gross **dereliction** of my duty. _______________________________

7. the same bland, polite, **obsequious** seaman of the voyage out. _______________________________
   ____

Comprehension Questions

Answer the following in complete sentences.

1. Describe Silver's final act as "double traitor."_______________________________
   ____
   ____
   ____
   ____

2. What is the reaction of the pirates to Silver's betrayal? _______________________________
   ____
   ____
   ____

3. Describe how Jim is saved. _______________________________
   ____
   ____
   ____

4. Who was the hero "from beginning to end"? Explain. _______________________________
   ____
   ____
   ____
   ____
   ____
   ____
   ____

5. What is the reaction of Jim's friends to Silver? ___________________________________

____

____

____

____

Quotations

Identify the speaker of the following.

"So you've changed sides again." ____

"One's the old cripple that brought us all here and blundered us down to this; the other's that cub that I mean to have the heart of." ____

"I reckon I settled you." ____

"But the dead men, sir, hang about your neck like mill-stones." ____

Discussion Questions

1. Who is the chieftain the chapter title refers to?

2. What does the squire mean when he says the dead men hang about Silver's neck like millstones?

3. Do you think anyone that hunted for the treasure deserved to find it? Explain.

Enrichment

1. Can you recall how many times Silver changed sides during the adventure? List his treacheries and their outcomes.

2. Draw a picture of Ben Gunn's cave as described in the book.

3. What is a *teetotum*? See if you can make one out of paper.

Vocabulary
Write the meaning of each bold word or phrase.

1. a strange collection, like Billy Bones's **hoard** for the diversity of coinage _____________________
    ____

2. he kept on trying to **ingratiate** himself with all. ____
    ____

3. with their arms raised in **supplication**. ____

4. what with **baffling** winds and a couple of fresh gales_______________________________________
    ____

5. he began, with wonderful **contortions**, to make us a confession __________________________
    ____

6. The maroon had **connived** at his escape in a shore boat _____________________________________
    ____

7. he still lives, a great favorite, though something of a **butt** _________________________________
    ____

Comprehension Questions
Answer the following in complete sentences.

1. Describe the battling emotions towards Silver that Jim feels. ___________________________
    ____
    ____
    ____
    ____

2. Describe how the men leave the remaining pirates on the island. _________________________
    ____
    ____
    ____
    ____
    ____

3. What happened to Silver? What do the men think of this?_______________________________

____

____

____

4. What are Jim's lingering dreams of the island? ____________________________________

____

____

Quotations

Identify the speaker of the following.

"You're the man to keep your word, we know that." _______________________________________

"Pieces of eight! Pieces of eight!" ____

Discussion Questions

1. Does Dr. Livesey's final comment about the remaining pirates surprise you? What would you have done?

2. Do you think Silver should have gone home free when the remaining crew was marooned?

3. Each man spent his share of the treasure "according to nature." Explain.

4. Were you satisfied with the ending of *Treasure Island*? How would you have changed the story?

Enrichment

1. Research the following types of coinage Jim sorts through: *moidores, sequins.*

2. Write your own alternate ending for *Treasure Island*, going as far back as you wish.

Drawing Page

Drawing Page

Appendix
of
Nautical
Terms

General Terms

A

abaft—in the direction of the stern
about—on the other tack
adrift—loose from the moorings
alee—when the helm is put over to leeward

B

batten—a thin strip of wood fitted into a pocket in the leach of a fore-and-aft sail to make the sail set better
bear down—to approach from windward
becalmed—said of a vessel when in a calm
belay—to make fast to a pin or cleat
belaying pin—a wooden or iron shape fitting into a rail, and used for securing gear
bilge—the curved part of the ship's hull where the sides and flat bottom meet
bill of exchange—a written agreement in which a debtor agrees to pay a creditor a specified sum on a specified date
boatswain (bosen)—a ship's petty officer in charge of the deck crew, boats, etc.
boom—a spar used for extending the foot of a fore-and-aft sail
bow—the forward part of a vessel's sides
bowsprit—a spar extending out from the stem and carrying the lead of part of the gear for the headsails
breach—seas that break entirely over a vessel
broach—to fly up into the wind unintentionally; to be thrown broadside on, in surf
bulkhead—transverse or longitudinal partition separating portions of the ship
bulwarks—the light plating or wooden extension of the ship's sides above the upper deck
by the board—overboard

C

canted—inclined
capsize—to overturn
capstan—an upright drum around which cables are wound so as to haul them in
capstan bar—a wooden bar used for heaving the capstan by hand
careen—to list or heel over
cat's paw—1. a double-looped knot formed by twisting two bights of rope—the hook of a tackle is passed through them
2. the slight ruffling of the surface of the water caused by passing flaws of wind in calm airs
clamp down—to sprinkle and swab down, as a deck in hot weather
clinch—a half-hitch (knot) stopped to its own part
close-hauled—sailing close to the wind; on the wind, or by the wind
close-reefed—a sail reduced to its smallest area (rolled up)
clove hitch—a bend formed by making two half-hitches about the spar for hitching ratlines to the shrouds
colors—the national ensign (flag)

coxswain (cosen)—the enlisted man in charge of a boat and usually serving as steersman
crossing the line—crossing the Equator

D

Davy Jones' Locker—the bottom of the sea
deadlight—round thick glass in the side of a ship for lighting purposes
dead reckoning—a navigator's reckoning with courses steered and distances run, independent of sights and bearings
derelict—an abandoned vessel at sea
doldrums—the belt on each side of the equator in which little or no wind ordinarily blows
douse—to take in, or lower, a sail; to put out a light; to cover with water
downhaul—a rope led from the head of a headsail and through a block at the foot of the stay for hauling down the sail
draw—a sail when bellied out by the wind
drift—the amount of leeway of a vessel, or of a tide or current

E

ensign—the national flag
even keel—floating level

F

fathom—six feet
fore-and-aft—from the bow to the stern, lengthwise, as in sails
forecastle—the upper deck forward of the foremast
forecastle deck—a partial deck at the bow over the main deck
forefoot—the heel of the stem where it connects to the keel

G

gaff—the spar to which the head of a fore-and-aft sail is secured
galley—the ship's kitchen
gallows—the framework sometimes fitted above the main or superstructure deck for boat stowage and for the stowage of spare parts
gangway—an opening in the bulwarks to give entrance to the ship; or in ships without bulwarks, the opening in the rail used for boarding or leaving the ship
ground swell—the swell encountered in shoal (shallow) water and which is constant
gunwale—the rail of a boat

H

handspike—a small wooden bar similar to a capstan or an anchor bar, used for prying
handy—a handy vessel is one which handles easily
hard-a-lee—to put the tiller all the way up
hatch—an opening in a ship's deck for communication or for handling stores or cargo
hawser—a large rope used for heavy work, such as towing
head—the ship's water closet (bathroom)
helm—the wheel or tiller by which a ship is steered
hold—the space below decks utilized for the stowage of ballast, cargo, and stores (and prisoners)

hulk—a worn-out and stripped vessel
hull—the frame or main body of a ship

J

jib—a headsail set on a stay forward of the foremast
jib-boom—a spar rigged out beyond the bowsprit and through the bowsprit cap
Jolly Roger—a pirate's flag carrying the skull and crossbones

K

keel—the timber or bar forming the backbone of the vessel and running from the stem to the sternpost at the bottom of the ship

L

landing strake—the second line of planking below the gunwale
lanyard—a rope made fast to an article for securing it (e.g., knife lanyard, bucket lanyard) or for setting up rigging
leeward—the direction away from the wind
list—the inclination of a vessel not caused by wind or sea
luff—the forward edge of a fore-and-aft sail
lug—to carry (as to lug sail)
lugger—a sailing vessel with quadrilateral fore-and-aft sails, the head carried on a hoisting yard, and the luff shorter than the leech

M

mainsail—the sail spread by the main gaff and boom
marlinspike—a pointed iron instrument used in working with rope and wire
mast—a vertical spar supporting the booms, gaffs, and sails
masthead—any portion of the upper 15 feet of the lower mast
mizzen—the third mast from forward of a vessel with more than two masts (middle)

N

netting—a rope network

P

pipe to—the boatswain's pipe call to an evolution (or series of tasks)

Q

quartermaster—a petty officer of the bridge force

R

ridgepole—the horizontal pole supporting the middle of an awning
rigging—ropes and chains for a ship's masts and sails
rudder—a flat wooden shape fitted on the sternpost by pintles swivelling in gudgeons, and for the purpose of steering the boat (i.e., the flat board that sits in the back of the boat in the water and steers the boat)

     Appendix of Nautical Terms

S

schooner—a sailing vessel with two or more masts with fore-and-aft sails and with head sails carried on a bowsprit and jib-boom

scud—low-lying mist clouds

scull—to propel a boat by working an oar from side to side over the stern

scuttle-butt—the container of fresh water for drinking purposes and used by the crew; formerly it consisted of a cask

sea-cock—a cock in a pipe connected to the sea; a vessel may be flooded by opening the sea-cock

sheet—the rope used to spread the clew of headsails and to control the boom of boom sails

shipping articles—the agreement of the ship's officers and the crew with the owners or agents (sign articles)

shipshape—neat, seamanlike

shore up—to prop up

shove off—to leave

shrouds—side stays of hemp or wire from the masthead to the rail and set up by dead-eyes

slip—to let go by unshackling, as of a cable

smart—snappy, seamanlike (a smart ship is an efficient one)

spar—a slender rod or pole (as a mast) supporting the sail of a ship

spyglass—a small hand telescope

stanchions—wooden or metal uprights used as supports

stern—the rear end of a ship

stern sheets—the space in a boat abaft the afterthwart

stow—to put in place

supercargo—a merchant vessel's officer charged with managing the ship's business

T

tack—to change from one tack to another by putting the helm down; close-hauled on the wind

tarpaulin—heavy canvas used as a covering

taut—with no slack; strict as to discipline

teeth—directly towards the wind

thwart—a seat across a boat on which a rower may sit

tiller—a short piece of iron or wood fitting into the rudder head and by which the rudder is turned

topmast—the mast next above the lower mast

top sides—above deck

W

weather—to windward

weather eye—(to keep a weather eye is to be on the alert)

weather gauge—the situation of a vessel to windward of another vessel

wide berth—at a considerable distance

windward—toward the wind

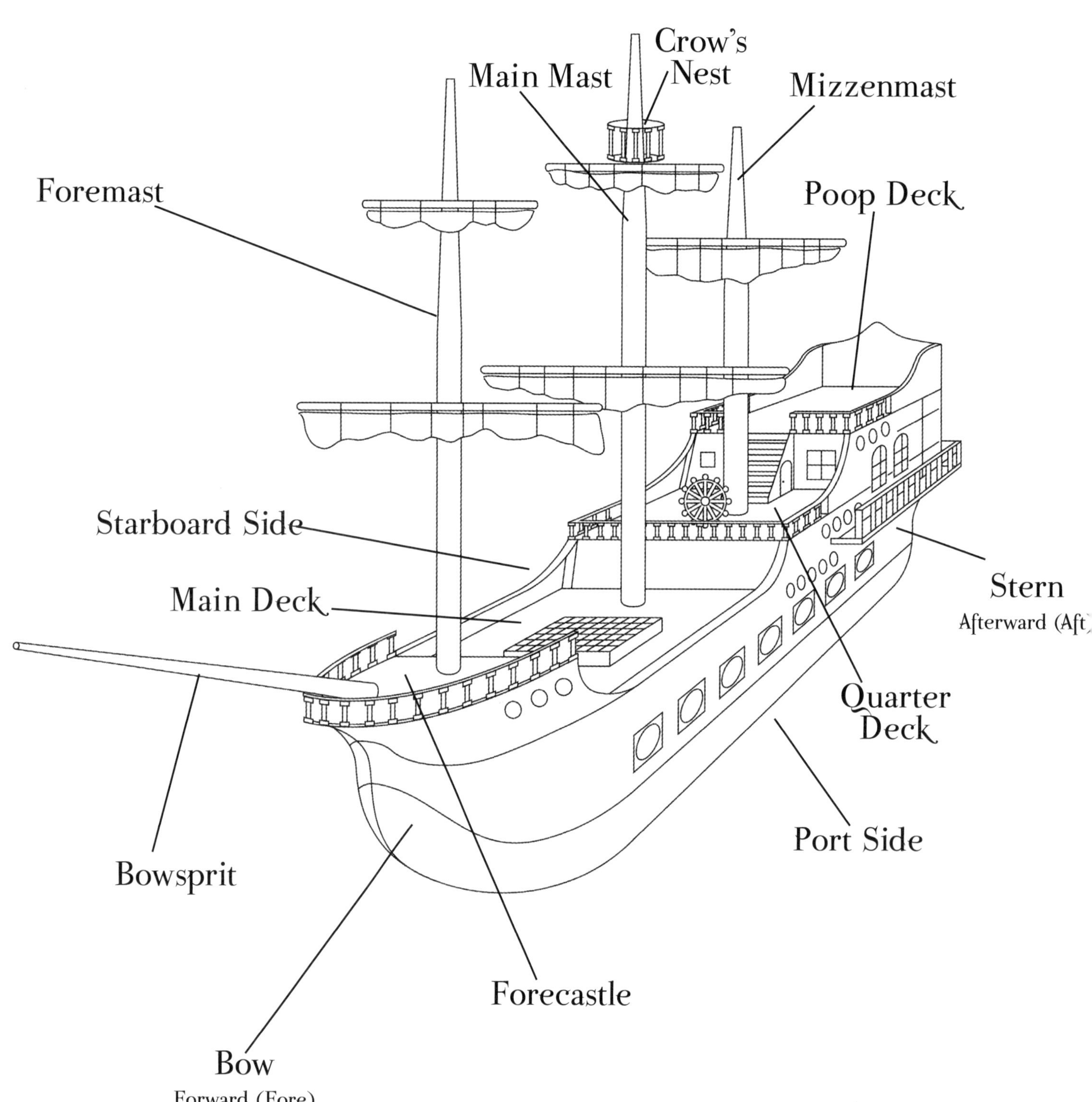

Foremast
Main Mast
Crow's Nest
Mizzenmast
Poop Deck
Starboard Side
Main Deck
Stern
Afterward (Aft)
Quarter Deck
Port Side
Bowsprit
Forecastle
Bow
Forward (Fore)

Parts of a Ship

bow—the forward part of a vessel's sides
bridge—a crosswise platform or enclosed area above the main deck of a ship from which the ship is controlled
brig—the ship's prison, formerly a sailor's slang phrase
cabin—the captain's quarters
crow's nest—the platform on the mast for the lookout
forecastle—the upper deck forward of the foremast
galley—the ship's kitchen
gallows—the framework sometimes fitted above the main or superstructure deck for boat stowage and for the stowage of spare parts
gunwale—the rail of a boat
head—the ship's water closet (bathroom)
helm—the wheel or tiller by which a ship is steered
hold—the space below decks utilized for storage
magazine—the space provided for the stowage of explosives
mast—a tall vertical pole (spar) used to support the sails and yards (horizontal poles) on a ship
rudder—a broad, flat, moveable piece hinged to the rear of a ship, used for steering
skids—beams sometimes fitted over the decks for the stowage of heavy boats
spar—a slender pole or rod supporting the sail of a ship
steerage—the junior officer's quarters
stern—the rear part of a ship
tiller—a short piece of iron or wood fitting into the rudder head and by which the rudder is turned
uptake—the enclosed trunk connecting a boiler or a group of boilers to the smoke stack

Sails and Parts of Sails

batten—a thin strip of wood fitted into a pocket in the leach of a fore-and-aft sail to make the sail set better
clew—the after lower corner of a fore-and-aft sail
foot—the lower edge of a sail
jib—a headsail set on a stay forward of the foremast
luff—the forward edge of a fore-and-aft sail
mainsail—the sail spread by the main gaff and boom
rigging—the ropes and chains for a vessel's masts and sails
tack—the lower forward corner of a fore-and-aft sail
topsail—a sail set over a lower sail
yard—a light spar to which the head of a lug rig sail is secured; in a square-rigged vessel, the spar suspended horizontally from the mast and to which the head of a square sail is bent

Boats and Ships

derelict—an abandoned vessel at sea
gig—a ship's boat designated for the use of a commanding officer
hulk—a worn-out and stripped vessel
lugger—a sailing vessel with quadrilateral fore-and-aft sails, the head carried on a hoisting yard, and the luff shorter than the leech
jolly boat—a small boat used in the merchant service and corresponding to a dinghy on a man-of-war
punt—a rectangular flat-bottomed boat, usually propelled by sculling and used for cleaning and painting the water line
schooner—a sailing vessel with two or more masts, with fore-and-aft sails and with head sails carried on a bowsprit and jib-boom

Ropes and Knots

bowline—a hitch in the form of a noose; used for securing hawsers to decks or moorings, and for lowering men over the side of a ship, etc.
cable—a rope; a chain secured to an anchor
cat's paw—a type of knot; a double-loop formed by twisting two bights of rope—the hook of a tackle is passed through them
clinch—a half-hitch (knot) stopped to its own part
clove hitch—a knot formed by making two half-hitches about the spar for hitching ratlines to the shrouds
cordage—a general term for rope of all kinds
hawser—a large rope used for heavy work, such as towing
junk—old rope
ratline stuff—small stuff (rope), three-stranded, right-handed, and tarred; used for rattling rigging
spun yarn—rough stuff made from long tow, laid up loosely left-handed of two, three, or four strands; used for seizings and small stuff
thrums—short strands of rope with strands unlaid and stuck through a mat to make a rough surface
yarn—1. twisted fibers (for rope) 2. tales—to "spin a yarn" is to tell a story

     Appendix of Nautical Terms

Wind and Sea, Directions, and Sailing Terms

abaft—by

about—on the other tack (or direction)

alee—when the helm is put over to leeward

all-aback—when all the sails are in stays (heavy rope or cable)

becalmed—said of a vessel when in a calm (no wind)

breach—seas that break entirely over a vessel

cat's paw—the slight ruffling of the surface of the water caused by passing flaws of wind in calm airs

close-hauled—sailing close to the wind

close-reefed—a sail reduced to its smallest area (rolled up)

draw—a sail when bellied out by the wind

drift—the amount of leeway of a vessel, or of a tide or current

fore-and-aft—-from the bow to the stern, lengthwise, as in sails

full spread—having all sails set

furl—to gather up and secure a sail

ground swell—the swell encountered in shoal (shallow) water and which is constant

hand—to furl a sail

haul to windward—to bring a vessel to the wind when sailing free

head to wind—the situation of a vessel in the eye of the wind

heave to—to bring a vessel's head to the wind and hold her there by the use of the sails

in stays—the situation of a vessel when coming about and the wind is spilled from the sails

larboard—port; left

leeward—away from the wind; the side or direction away from the wind

lie—the same as "heave to"

luff her—an order to bring the vessel into the wind by putting the helm down

mend—to refurl a sail which has been improperly furled

port—the left side of a ship; to turn the helm to the port side; an opening in the ship

scudding—driving before a gale

starboard—to steer right; right side of the ship

trades—the practically steady winds found in the Tropics and blowing towards the Equator

teeth—directly towards or into the wind

weather tide—a tide setting to windward

windward—towards the wind; the side or direction from which the wind blows